SUDDENLY HOME

A QUICK START GUIDE TO SUCCESSFULLY
WORKING FROM HOME

BETH DETJENS

For my friend and mentor, Kathy, who first afforded me the opportunity to work from home...

For my amazing supervisor, Zebrah, for mastering the art of working from home and for so graciously leading others who work remotely...

For all of my work-from-home friends and the families who tolerate us...

For my family, who are a constant source of stress, frustration, and unconditional love and support...

1

HOW DID I GET HERE?

I've heard the frustrations of so many friends newly assigned to work from home as a result of the COVID-19 pandemic in 2020. Many said they had always wanted the opportunity to work from home — until they suddenly had no other option. They quickly learned that managing an in-home office in the midst of running a household is not for the faint of heart.

When I transitioned to working from home almost 20 years ago, it was a novel idea not widely embraced by most employers. I hadn't even considered it until it was offered to me as an alternative to resigning my position to be a stay-at-home mom. Here's how my work-from-home transition went.

"I'M SO SORRY, but I just don't think I'll be coming back to work after all." That's what I intended to say when I walked into my boss's office to resign after my son was born in 2003. Though I did begin our conversation that way, I ended it with a promise to consider the incredible offer my boss had made. Work from home.

The company I worked for employed approximately 500 employees and operated offices in four states. I was a marketing executive and my primary function was technical writing. It was a position that could be done from anywhere as long as there was a good internet connection.

Only one other employee at my company had worked from home before me and thankfully, she did an amazing job. She proved conclusively that working from home could be done and done well. Because of her success, my employer was willing to let me try it instead of losing me altogether to motherhood.

I came back the next day with a clear goal in mind — to minimize my time in the office and maximize my time at home with my new baby. We landed on a two-week trial period, during which I would work from home three days a week and come into the office the other two days. If that worked well, we would reduce the in-office days to one and then to none.

I arranged for a babysitter on the days I had to go into the office, because my husband also worked full-time as a college instructor. I set up my home office the

way I thought it would work best, and I traded my desktop computer in my work office for a laptop with a docking station. I was ready. Or at least I thought I was ready.

The first day was heaven. Without the additional time required for hair, makeup, dressing in office attire and getting my baby to the sitter on time, I gained a solid hour and a half in the morning and still started my workday on time. By 8:00am, I was on my second cup of coffee, sitting in my home office working like a maniac. My son, Devin, was still asleep because I hadn't yanked him from his crib an hour and a half ago to get ready for his day at the sitter.

I could totally do this.

Even when Devin woke up, I was still able to work with practically no interruption. I simply moved my laptop to the kitchen table, so I could work while feeding him breakfast. I took a short break to read to him, play with some toys, and before I knew it, he was ready for a nap. By the time he woke from his nap two hours later, I had completed the better part of my workday. In fact, I had accomplished more in that two hours than I normally did in four hours at the office.

I'd earned a long lunch break. Because I was home, I cooked a hot meal (soup and grilled cheese) and ate an unhurried lunch with the cutest lunch date. Devin reacted well to the extra time with me and played contentedly while I finished up my work for the day. I was done with an extra hour left over.

We had time for a walk before I started dinner and I started to believe I could actually be the attentive stay-at-home mom that I wanted to be, while still being the rock-star-employee that I needed to be. A few hours later my husband, Derrek, arrived home from work to a calm, happy family and a delicious meal. He probably thought he was in the wrong house. I told him how I'd accomplished a full 8-hour workday and had plenty of time with Devin. We celebrated this exciting new chapter for our family.

Day 1 had been a whopping success. But Day 2 was coming...

∽

I WAS SO PUMPED from the success of my first day working from home that I created a schedule for Devin and me. Derrek left for work at 7:00am and didn't get home until 7:00pm due to a long commute, so it was mostly just the two of us. In addition to my 8-hour workday, I'd scheduled mini-breaks for myself throughout the day so I could spend quality time with my baby. My one-hour lunch break I would have had in the office became four mini-breaks of 15 minutes each. I grazed on food throughout the day while I worked and played to make up the time, which I could do since I was at home all day with my own kitchen.

The first mini-break of the day was for Devin's wake-up routine of dressing, breakfast, and playtime. The second was for enrichment with either art or music. The third was a reading break right before his big nap. And the fourth was a late afternoon play break either inside or out, depending on the weather.

If you're a parent, you're likely laughing hysterically at the idea that a new mom would ever expect to have such control over a baby's schedule. I quickly learned otherwise on Day 2.

When the time came for the first mini-break, Devin's morning routine, he was sound asleep so we skipped it. That worked fine for Devin, but it pushed his wake-up time (which he announced ever so loudly) to the dead center of my first at-home teleconference. I learned you only look for the mute button on your phone once, because every time after that your finger hovers very near it during entire meetings. I finished that meeting by letting him nurse while I typed with one hand and discovered the perfect pairing of the speaker button and the mute button on my phone.

Not ideal, but we were coping.

The second mini-break was a success and Devin happily played in his pack-and-play in the living room by me while I worked on my laptop. I was so busy on a project deadline, however, that I completely missed his nap time. Uh-oh. I had a feeling I would pay dearly for that. In too deep with my task at hand, I decided to push through and race my baby's missed-nap rage to the finish line. All I had to do was finish this project by the deadline before Devin got cranky enough to require my attention. I almost made it.

At 3:00pm, he got fussy. At 3:30pm, he got angry. At 4:00pm, he got sleepy. No, no, no! I couldn't let him fall asleep this late or we'd never sleep through the night. I was so close to done with this project too.

They say necessity is the mother of invention. How else would I have come up with the first standing desk I'd ever heard of? I placed my laptop on the kitchen counter and for the next two hours I typed while I held and bounced Devin, keeping him active enough with toys that he couldn't fall asleep so close to bedtime.

Finally, I did it. I submitted my final project with an hour to spare and Devin was...

...asleep. What?! How did I miss that? I looked at the clock and realized I'd worked straight through all of our mini-breaks. I'd completed my workday successfully, but Devin had missed his nap and now would be awake half the night.

Day 3 was not looking good.

～

WHAT WAS I thinking when I agreed to this crazy work-from-home idea? I know what I was thinking. I was thinking of Day One in all its glory. Day Two had been a rude awakening and Day Three was shaping up to be a repeat with the added bonus of a sleepless night with my late-napping boy. What was I missing?

It took awhile for us to find our groove and establish a work-from-home dynamic that worked well. When we did, the result was a stunning success. I quickly realized that I could complete twice as much work at home in half the time it would have taken in an office setting. On the rare occasions that I did work in the office, I wondered how on earth anyone gets anything done there.

For the next almost 20 years, I've worked exclusively from home and can't imagine working any other way. For the first few years, I had the same boss and we enjoyed a mutual and productive understanding of the type of leadership that would extract my highest quality work product and lowest stress level. I've had several other supervisors since her, and some understood better than others. But, even with the most challenging of all these supervisors, working from home was the magic ingredient that made it possible for me to do my best work with the best work-life balance.

2

STEP 1: PREPARATION

Do you remember your reaction when you heard the news that you were going to work from home for the foreseeable future? If it was the result of the COVID-19 pandemic, you may have been among the millions of Americans suddenly placed in a position that either thrilled you or terrified you. Either way, you probably could have benefited from some seasoned advice on how to set yourself up for success.

The first and most obvious question to answer is, "Where in my house will I work?"

~

Set Yourself Up For Success

If you're like most people, your house may not have a well-appointed office space already set up with privacy from clingy children, noisy pets, and the everyday demands of your home. So, let's start with an office space.

Unless you have an extra room waiting to be used as an office, you may need to think outside the box. Where in your home could you set up a desk big enough for the necessities — your laptop, chargers, lamp, and room to place a few desk accessories or files? It doesn't have to be fancy, but it should be in a quiet place where you can concentrate.

You're going to be spending several hours a day in this space, so don't forget about ergonomics. Your monitor (or laptop screen) should be at eye level so you don't strain your neck looking up or down. When your hands are on your keyboard, your arms should be at a 90-degree angle with your wrists relaxed and comfortably at rest on the keyboard.

In your office at work, did you use multiple monitors on your desk? You can quickly create the same efficiency in your home office. If your employer isn't able to provide you an extra computer monitor for your home office, don't worry. That smart TV by your desk will work beautifully. Depending on the type of computer you have, you may not even need to use a cord. Most current laptops have a built-in ability to wirelessly cast what's on the screen to another display.

You can choose whether to simply mirror your laptop's screen to the larger screen (in this case, your smart TV) or extend your desktop to use both screens. Either way, the extra real estate will mean far less switching between open windows and possibly much greater productivity.

If you don't have a desk chair you love, now is the time to invest in one. If a new chair isn't an option, use pillows to adapt a chair you have to be seated at the right height with plenty of lumbar support. Sit toward the front of your chair so you have an inch or two between the front edge of your chair and the back of your knees. If you need ergonomic adjustments, ask your employer. You may be surprised how willing they may be to ship you whatever you need.

Make your desk an inspiring space you can enjoy — as much as anyone can enjoy work. Add a splash of your favorite color, place a pretty plant on the desk, pick out your favorite coffee mug, or whatever it takes to make the space your own. And if there's no room for a desk, consider adapting a kitchen island, high-top dining table, or other raised countertop to be a standing desk. Just remember to place your screen at the right height to practice good ergonomics.

～

Set Some Expectations

Next, you'll need to set up some ground rules for the family. Whether you have kids at home who need you throughout the day, or you live in relative peace and quiet, you'll need to build in some structure and set everyone's expectations in advance. It may be a good idea to tell friends and family what hours each day that you plan to work so they can avoid calling or texting then — or at least know why you didn't respond if you miss a call or text while working.

To set some expectations for yourself, consider adding a few recurring reminders on your phone or computer calendar so you don't work through lunch or forget a time-sensitive task. Especially if you're a task-oriented person who gets lost in their work, make breaks a priority, even if it's just a five-minute stretch every hour or so. If your smart watch is as annoying as mine, you'll get all the reminders you need to move once in awhile. Just don't ignore them as much as I do.

~

Schedule Your Workday

Now you have your office space and a little structure to keep work at "work" (which is now home) and home at home, where it's always been. To make it all function, you'll likely need some sort of schedule.

To get started, consider your work-in-the-office daily schedule. What time did you start your day? What time did you get home from work? How did you transition from "work mode" to "home mode"? To ease the transition to your new normal, it may be helpful to follow that schedule as much as possible. If you got up to work out before getting ready for work, do that. If you didn't check your work email from home once you left work, don't check them after your home workday ends.

For the days that you have to go somewhere at a certain time, add it to your calendar and always have a back-up plan in mind, just in case a work meeting runs long or a deadline crops up unexpectedly.

On my daily calendar, I have recurring time slots blocked off for a quick stretch every two hours, a 15-minute break at 4:00pm to prep dinner, a reminder to stop working at 5:00pm to cook, and of course, reminders for all of the work meetings I have throughout the day. If I have any errands, I plan them for my lunch hour and put it on my work calendar with the time marked as "busy" or "out-of-office" so no-one books me for a meeting at that time.

～

Set Aside Time for Family and Friends

Make sure your family and friends know when you're available and when you're not. If you have pets at home, plan for the inevitable barking when the mailman comes or when the doorbell rings. Better yet, turn the doorbell off if you can.

The most important advice I can give you is some that I rarely take myself. You have to actually stop working at the end of the workday and be with your family. I know you may think that sounds crazy, but when work is always there and your family is always there, you have to make a conscious choice every day. When my son was about to turn two, he taught me this when he walked over to me, took the laptop out of my hands, and said, "I don't like this thing." Out of the mouths of babes...

We know that family comes first, but sometimes a project deadline has other plans. On those days, take an hour or so to be with the family, have dinner, help with homework, or whatever they need from you. Then hop back on your computer to finish your work after the kids are in bed, or while the rest of the family cleans the kitchen. You probably don't want to make a habit of working late, but sometimes work happens.

Most importantly, don't give into guilt. It's easy to feel like you're always losing — when you're working you're not there for your family and when you're with your family you're not there for work. You'll never get it right all of the time and you have to be okay with that. Just do the best you can and let the rest go. Tomorrow is another day.

∾

Plan Ahead

From childcare to meal planning, a little planning can go a long way. Do yourself a favor and get as much help as you can from friends and family for childcare. Maybe your sister can give your kids a ride home from school and help with homework one or two days a week. If so, schedule your most intense meetings or work tasks for those time slots.

Do you like to cook but lack the time? Use the weekend to do the prep work for the week's meals — plan your menu, do the grocery shopping, and put everything together that you can — including a week's worth of lunches for yourself. And don't forget to prepare plenty of grab-and-go snacks that are high in protein and low in sugar. You'll need all the fuel you can get and nobody has time for a sugar crash in the afternoon.

This may also be an ideal time to make use of some conveniences like grocery delivery, Walmart pick-up, and the carpool for getting your kids to and from school with minimal interruptions. Just be sure to block off the time on your work calendar when you're the driver for carpool.

The big idea here is to think through everything in your week that's predictable. Write it all down and plan your workday around those things. For example, if your kids are at school from 8am until 3pm every day, schedule meetings during that time. If you know you are most alert and focused in the morning, plan you most challenging work for that time and save the light-weight tasks for the late afternoon when the kids are home from school and you're not at your best. You get the idea.

~

Home Office Checklist

By this point, you may have already completed many of the steps we've touched on in this "Preparation" chapter. Before we move on to "Performance," let's make sure you're set up for success.

- Designate your office space **location**.
- **Arrange** your office space (e.g., lighting, ergonomics, equipment, etc.).
- Set up any **planning tools** needed (e.g., dry

erase boards, bulletin board, meal calendar, desk supplies, etc.).

- Communicate the **ground rules and expectations** for your availability to family and friends.
- Secure any **help** you need for childcare, meal planning, etc.
- Set recurring **calendar reminders** for breaks, lunch, errands, appointments, and the end of your workday.
- Establish your **daily schedule** (e.g., wake time, stop time, etc.).
- Communicate any **needs or concerns** to your supervisor (e.g., equipment needed, ergonomic accommodations needed, etc.)

3

STEP 2: PERFORMANCE

The name of the game here is making sure you have what you need, where you need it, when you need it so you can get things **done**. In the previous chapter, you set up your workspace, so everything should be reasonably functional for you by this point. Now we want to shift our focus to Step 2 — getting results by doing an awesome job — yes, even from home.

～

Stay Connected

Remember, all these messaging platforms serve another purpose beyond the monotony of work tasks. When you're working remotely, out of sight is out of mind. To stay in front of your colleagues, send each of your team members an email, instant message, or text at least once a week. If you don't have a work task to talk about, just take the time to say hi and check in with them. Not only is this friendly, it's a great way to get to know the people with whom you work.

If you're on a team with remote employees, make as many of your meetings as possible video conferences. So much is lost in translation on an audio-only conference call, and sometimes serious misunderstandings are the result. Take advantage of the available technology to really engage with your team and communicate at a higher level.

Whether you love it or hate it, technology is the remote employee's best friend. It's your lifeline to your work team, to your supervisor, and to all the tools that make your job not just possible, but also productive. It's what keeps you present with your team when you can't be there in person.

So, use the technology available to you to stay connected. What communication tools do you have in addition to email? Does your company use an instant messaging platform? Text messaging? Whatever you have, use it. The key is knowing when to use each.

- **Email:** Send an email when you need to communicate **detailed information that isn't overly time-sensitive.** If it is time-sensitive, be sure to clearly state any deadlines in the message. Never use all-caps (no-one wants to be yelled at), but limited use of bold, italics, underline or a bright color to accentuate key phrases — and deadlines — can be a huge time-saver for busy colleagues reading your email.

- **Instant Messaging:** Ping a colleague on IM **when you need — as the name implies — an instant reply.** This can be a lifesaver when deadlines are tight on a project or task. An average expectation for email is that it will be received and read within a few hours, whereas an instant message is — well — instant.

- **Text Messaging:** Texting is ideal **when you need a quick response and the recipient is likely away from their desk.** Travel is a great example. If your colleague is en route to a business meeting, texting may be the only way to get an immediate reply.

- **Voicemail or Voice Memos:** Recordings are perfect **when you need to communicate something complex or that could easily be misunderstood in written communication.** Before the days of voice memos, we accomplished this by calling a colleague to tell them, "I'm going to call you right back for a long voicemail, so don't answer when I call back. Okay?" Now, we can just record a voice memo in our texting app on the phone, or in any of the many other apps for this purpose. This is also a great option for providing a detailed update to a group of people involved in the subject of your voice memo. It may even take the place of a meeting if the purpose is simply to provide an update.

～

The Power of a Well-Written Email

Whichever method you use, your writing should be clear and concise. When you worked in an office, email was just one means of communication you used. If an email needed clarification, you could pop into the recipient's office for a quick connection on the messaging and all was well. Or maybe that face-to-face conversation would mean you didn't need to send the email at all.

Now that you're working from home, the quality and effectiveness of your emails is more important than ever. It's your primary means of communication and it can make or break your productivity.

To help with that, here are a few tips and tricks I've

picked up along the way for writing emails that are read, understood and get results:

- **Keep it classy.** Write like the professional you are.
- **Keep it clear.** Limit yourself to one key topic per email if possible. Use bullets to break down complex sentences into easily digestible messages a recipient can understand at a glance.
- **Keep it quick.** Statistically speaking, your message will get only a few seconds of the recipient's time. Long messages get skimmed at best, which leads to misunderstanding, missing details and a general mess.

Have you ever gotten an email at work that you had to read more than once to figure out what in the world the sender wanted you to do? When you worked in an office, a misinterpreted email might be a rare instance. When your communication is exclusively by email, instant message, or text, the likelihood of your emails being misread increases exponentially. What does that mean for you?

It means you have to be extra careful with every message. If you're worried the extra attention to detail will add time you don't have to an already busy workday, don't. By investing a few extra seconds when you write each email, you'll avoid hours or even days of extra work that can result from a poorly-communicated message.

For example, imagine that you're emailing a colleague in another department to give them direction on a project to which you've both been assigned. You've received new information from the client that will change the course of the project and you're communicating the news internally. Consider the outcome of each scenario:

- **Scenario 1:** You're in a huge hurry, running late to a meeting, and you punch out a quick email to your project teammate in the IT Department, telling her that the client wants the new technology to include an app-based user interface. Your teammate gets the message, assembles her team for a strategy session and they spend the next two days building an app interface before the next weekly project meeting.
- **Scenario 2:** You're still running late to that meeting, but you take an extra moment to re-read the client's email. You see that his direction was for the user interface to **not** be app-based. You quickly but carefully

write an email to your teammate with the
new information.

In Scenario 1, you wasted two full days of the
project timeline on a task that the client specifically
did not want. In Scenario 2, you sent a clearly-worded
email that kept the project on track. I've learned first-
hand that it takes less time to do something right the
first time than to clean up a mess created from poor
communication.

~

The "RE" Rules of Email

Wait. This is a book about working from home. Why
are you telling me how to write an email? We all know
how to do that.

Yes, you're absolutely right. But when you work
from home, email becomes far more important to you.
Now you can't follow-up face-to-face, catch up with
colleagues in the break room, or chat in the conference
room before or after a meeting. When you're working
from home, email (and instant messaging or texting) is
more important than ever, so you'll need to be at the
top of your communication game.

Think of this as the "RE" rules of email.

- **Re**view the information you'll be communicating in your email. It may be an email you received, a conversation you had with someone, or just an idea you had. Whatever it is, take the time to process it fully before you ever write a word.

- **Re**-write your first attempt if it's not crystal clear. Take the extra second to clean up the phrasing, put ideas in the right order, make sure you have covered all the information without cluttering your message with unrelated details.

- **Re**-read your email draft as if you're the recipient — before sending it. Pretend you only know as much about the topic as the recipient knows. If they read that email, would they understand what you're trying to communicate? If not, clean it up.

The same rule applies for replying to emails. You should always read the entire email and really process it before beginning your reply. I've found that most misinterpreted emails are the direct result of someone just not reading the email — or not reading it carefully. One of my favorite supervisors always said, "Over-communicate. Even if you *think* you've communicated it enough, you haven't."

4

STEP 3: PRODUCTIVITY

Let's say you have your work space all set up and you've modified your work day to accommodate all the distractions of home. You've established your team's expectations, your family's expectations and your own and you're ready to produce phenomenal results.

How? How about a few time-tested tricks of the trade? In working exclusively from home since 2003, I've tried just about every tool, hack and suggestion out there. Obviously, what worked for me won't work for everyone since we're all unique. I learned that when my husband, Derrek, started working from home. Our work styles were completely opposite.

This difference in work styles is most evident in our home office setup. My preferred workspace — by far — is the most comfortable chair possible. In our home, that seat is the reclining section of our leather sofa. My "desk" is the end table and ottoman beside the couch and my computer is a laptop that is literally on my lap all day (it sits on an ergonomically-correct lap desk that Derrek found on Amazon).

Derrek's preferred workspace is an actual office in the house with a door that closes, a real desk, two monitors plugged into his laptop's docking station, and all of the usual office supplies. He wakes up at the same time every day, follows the same morning routine, and even dresses for work.

But your work style goes way beyond seating and desk setup. You have to figure out all the dynamics in your workspace that will empower you to unleash your best work self. For example, if I work in a silent room, my mind wanders and it takes effort to focus.

I've learned that the most effective way for me to stay on the task at hand is to have music or something on in the background. I don't even pay attention to the noise. I just need to distract myself from where I am — with what I'm doing. When my surroundings become white noise, I'm 100% in the zone and I lock into what I'm doing with laser focus.

Our kids have learned our work styles well. If they need to slip something past us — like permission to do something we normally wouldn't approve — they'll wait until I'm in the zone and ask me. When I later object to whatever it is that I supposedly agreed to when I was working, I won't even remember the conversation.

Derrek is totally different. He'll listen to music, but he can also work in complete silence. And here's the best part — neither of our work styles is wrong. They're both right as long as they achieve the desired result.

I also believe there are certain work styles that make working from home difficult if not impossible. One of my dearest friends took a position in a company that was exclusively work-from-home and realized that she simply hates working from home. She found that she needs the in-office camaraderie, community, and face-to-face interactions with colleagues throughout the day.

Another challenging work style that I believe will find working from home difficult is the person who needs constant direction and motivation from a supervisor and peers in the office. In a home office, this person will soon find themselves wandering aimlessly, feeling overwhelmed ill-equipped to complete the tasks at hand.

∾

Master Your Work-From-Home Style

So, how do you identify your work-from-home style if you've never had the opportunity to do it before? One way is to imagine you have an entire day at home to accomplish a single project. What would you do?

Would you dive right in as soon as you woke up, tackle the project one step at a time and push yourself to have it all done by a certain time? Or would you figure out what the latest possible start time is and go from there? Would you see a sock on the floor and throw in a load of laundry? Would you see a cup on the counter and clean the whole kitchen? These answers are great clues to identifying your work-from-home style.

If you learn that you would use housekeeping to procrastinate your work, work in an area where you won't see the clutter. If you learn that you need a quiet area free from distractions, your workspace should reflect that. Pick an area least likely to be invaded by noisy family members. Adjust the lighting and air flow if needed to make your work the focus. The key is to assess your work style, own it, and optimize it.

$\sim$

Tools of the (Work-From-Home) Trade

Once you've set up your home office structure and schedule, you can dive into the wonderful world of tools that make remote work so rewarding and productive. If you're not a huge technology fan, you can adapt your favorite tech tools to a more comfortable version. For example, if you find a great scheduling app but don't want to use your phone all day for it, take the content you like from the app and turn it into a dry erase board version or a Pinterest-style bulletin board and make it work for you.

Task management tools are a lifesaver. For some, tasks are best managed from the tools on a mobile phone, voice-enabled virtual assistants, or computer. For others, it may be a Post-It note on the computer screen each day or a checklist. Whatever it is, put it front-and-center and use it every day. You may soon find that you've taken your work performance to a whole new level and can't imagine how you ever got anything done in a busy office.

One particularly powerful tool you may want in your arsenal is the customized routine feature that most mobile phones and virtual home assistants have. For example, you can program Bixby on your Samsung Galaxy phone to record a customized routine. With just a single command, like "Start my workday", your phone can enable silent notifications, start preset timers and reminders for work breaks and other scheduled tasks, and even send text messages to pre-selected recipients reminding them that you're at work.

A pre-set routine to end your day might include playing a celebratory song from your favorite playlist, sending text messages to pre-selected recipients that you're off work, and even opening your favorite app for recipes.

One of the most helpful tools in your arsenal may be the voice-activated assistant sitting on your shelf. If you haven't already, I recommend you read the instruction manual and use those devices to their full potential. Use the customizable routines on Alexa, Google Home devices, or whatever you have, to make your life a little easier.

Even low-tech tools can have a huge impact on your day. Think about your office setup and what was helpful to you there. Did you have a dry erase board on your office wall that you depended on? Hang one up in your home office area and set it up the same way.

What was on your office desk that you used? Are you a Post-It note fan? Do you have a favorite pen or highlighter? Set up your desk the way you like it and you'll feel right at home. At work. At home.

~

Dress for Success

Many of my smartest and most productive work-from-home friends swear by this next one — get dressed. It sounds simple but for many people the simple act of getting dressed as if you're going into the office resets your mind into work mode. It also signals a clear end to your workday when you change out of your "work clothes".

You don't have to go overboard, of course. Even changing from pajamas into casual clothes may be enough distinction to switch into work mode for you. Or go full office mode if that's your jam. I'll be over here in my loungewear because that's what works for me.

~

Silence, Please

Whether you prefer to work in silence or with all the noises of home around you, when it comes to phone calls, the rule is silence. Even if the person you're talking knows you work from home, the sound of your barking dog or screaming toddler communicates that you're not fully there. Sure, it's inevitable that once in awhile a sound will slip between you and the mute button, but the less frequent the better.

How do you make it sound like you're in an office in a building alone when you're home surrounded by chaos? One of the first phrases both of my kids probably learned was, "Shhhh. I'm in a meeting." To this day, when I say that, they are instantly silent and will write me a note or send a text with what they wanted to tell me.

I'm not sure exactly how they learned that lesson so well. I suppose it was the product of growing up as my officemate from birth all the way up. It's just how it always was for them. I remember explaining it to them as toddlers this way:

> "Do you remember what it's like in the office when we stop by to see Mommy's friends? You know how quiet it is and everyone is sitting at their desks all quiet and serious? If you came to visit me in my office at work, you'd have to be really quiet when Mommy was talking to her work friends. So when the phone rings or I'm in a meeting, we have to pretend that we're all there at work together."

That made it more of a game for them. And it worked. Rewards for being quiet during work phone calls and meetings helped too.

If your kids are younger or you have noisy pets, the mute button on your phone is your best friend. Keep one ear tuned to the soundtrack of your home to anticipate the next noise and one finger hovering over the mute button. If you're on the phone at the time your mail comes every day, distract the dog before the mail carrier arrives, by letting him or her play in the backyard (if it's fenced) or have a snack ready for the dog. After all, your dog can't bark with your mouth full of food.

If you're on the phone when it's time for your toddler to wake from his nap, have a sippy cup or a snack ready to hand them before they can cry. For this and for so many daily tasks at home, wireless ear buds connected to your phone can be a lifesaver. But first, get really familiar with how to answer calls, hang up and definitely how to mute.

~

Meetings

My first rule for meetings is don't have them — well, unless it's absolutely necessary. I can't count the number of meetings I've attended that should have been an email. Even though meetings are just a phone call or video conference from home, they're time-consuming and often not necessary at all. I've found two key methods for limiting the number of meetings that eat up your busy workday.

If you're about to schedule a meeting, first ask yourself these three questions:

- **Why am I scheduling this meeting?** Is it to inform or update a group of people about a situation or project? Or is it to actively discuss strategies, action items, and collaborate on a specific topic? If it's just to inform or update, write a good quality email with the information and call it a day. If you need to discuss something with a group, then schedule your meeting.
- **Who actually needs to attend this meeting?** I know it's tempting to click on so many people's names in the attendee column, but think about how many meetings are already on those people's calendars. If they're invited just to be a fly on the wall or to stay in the loop, do everyone a favor and just email the meeting notes to those folks after the meeting as an FYI. At the very least, invite them as an "optional" attendee so they can skip your meeting if needed.
- **How long do I really need for this meeting?** If you look at your work calendar, probably most of the meetings on it are scheduled for one hour. But how many of

those should have been shorter? A lot. To save everyone time when I'm scheduling meetings, I plan on 30 minutes as my default and only go to one hour when absolutely necessary. To give everyone a little cushion between back-to-back meetings, I suggest booking 20 minutes on the calendar for a 30-minute meeting and book 45 minutes on the calendar for a one-hour meeting. It pushes everyone to stay on task and you all get back precious time in your day for a quick refill on coffee, bathroom break, or even time to grab a healthy snack.

If you're invited to attend a meeting, you have a little less control, but there are still plenty of ways to limit your time in them. Here are a few of my favorites:

- **Request the notes.** If you're not instrumental to the discussion and were invited by default, reply "Tentative" instead of "Accept" or "Decline". This gives you the opportunity to reply to the sender in an email of your own. Use that vehicle to tell the meeting organizer that your time is limited and to ask if your attendance is critical. If it's not, ask them for a copy of the meeting notes, including any action items that may be assigned to you or your team.

- **Send a representative.** If the meeting isn't regarding a priority topic or a time-sensitive task, ask if you can send a representative to take notes for you and speak on your behalf. You may be surprised how well you can predict what questions or information other departments have for you and your team. Arm your representative with all of the information they need to answer basic questions and advise them to bring anything more complex back to you for a direct answer via email. This is also a great training opportunity for upcoming leaders on your team.

～

Video Conferences

When it comes to meetings, you may find it helpful to include the word "video" in the subject or notes for any video conferences so they don't catch you off-guard. If you're the meeting organizer, your attendees will appreciate the heads-up so they can plan to be video-ready and avoid being caught off-guard. If you do find yourself face-to-face with an unexpected video conference, here are a few rescue tips you can try.

- Keep a scarf and a jacket/sweater within arm's reach. You can throw them on over a T-shirt or even pajamas for a quick work look at a moment's notice.
- No makeup, no problem! Keep a lip gloss and a pair of reading glasses on your desk. The glasses will hide the fact that you're not wearing any eye makeup and the lip gloss will make you look put together, while taking the attention off of your hair and the rest of your face.
- Use the "touch-up-my-appearance" tool that most video conferencing apps have. It gives you just enough blur to airbrush away any imperfections.
- When possible, raise the camera on your computer so that you're looking slightly up at the camera instead of down. It will give you a slimmer and more awake look even if you just realized five minutes ago that this was a video conference.
- Set your video conferencing default to start without video. That will give you a few precious seconds to get yourself together before turning on your camera.

~

Don't Stress About the Mess

People used to tell me, "Oh, you work from home. I bet your house is immaculate." Clearly, these people thought my employer was paying me to clean house and not perform at the top of my game in the workplace. If you're a person who can't stand messes, I suggest you look the other way and don't stress about the mess. If there are house things that have to be done — laundry started, dinner prepped, etc. — use your lunch break for that or one of your 15-minute breaks in the morning or afternoon.

If you allow housework to creep into your workday, it can quickly take up far more time than you planned. What started as a quick load of laundry may end up an hour later as a reorganized dresser, clean floors and who knows what else. That isn't fair to your employer and it isn't in your best interest either. You may have a productive morning cleaning your house, but good luck doing a full day's work in just an afternoon — especially if your family is home and hungry by then.

~

Give Yourself a Break

Seriously. Take a break. In all the stress of adjusting to remote work, don't miss the unique opportunities of being at home. A 15-minute break in the office might have been a trip to the break room and bathroom, but at home that 15 minutes might be a walk around the block or story time with your little ones. If the weather's nice, open your windows and enjoy your home. Did you even have a window in your office space? Take that 15 minutes to do some yoga stretches. You can't wear yoga pants to work but you can at home. So take advantage of it.

Look around you and count your blessings. You have a job. You have a home. And now you don't even have to leave one to get to the other. Now go show your employer you can be a rockstar employee from anywhere. You can do it!

ABOUT THE AUTHOR

I've done my best to share what has worked for me and for others I know who work from home. But, there is so much more to learn, especially since everyone is so unique. I believe that the longer you work from home, the more you'll learn about what works best for you.

The key to mastering your new workspace is recognizing that the best strategies are the ones that make you feel the most focused and productive.

As you continue to navigate your new space, I'd love to hear from you on my website (bethdetjens.com). Use the "Ask the Author" area to contact me directly with your questions or ideas, or comment on the blog posts at my website whenever you have something to contribute.

You may even be interested in participating on the development of my next book, which takes a much deeper dive into the work-from-home styles I touched on in this book. If so, join my mailing list on the website to get updates on upcoming surveys and opportunities to share your insight on working from home.

Until then, I'm sending you all my encouragement as you make the best of being "suddenly home."

ALSO BY BETH DETJENS

Never Buy a Raccoon at a Gas Station

Never Put an Alligator in Your Car

Never Hide a Horse in the Freezer

The Complete Never Series: Books 1-3: Life Lessons for
Children of All Ages

www.ingramcontent.com/pod-product-compliance
Lightning Source LLC
Chambersburg PA
CBHW030535210326
41597CB00014B/1155